The All American Chili Cookbook

The Best Regional & Specialty Chili Recipes

Copyright Material

© 2023 James Masters

All Rights Reserved

No part of this book may be used or transmitted in any form or by any means without the proper written consent of the publisher and copyright owner, except for brief quotations used in a review. This book should not be considered a substitute for medical, legal, or other professional advice.

Sign-up Now
and Be Notified of New Books

Website: readbooks.today

email: juliette@readbooks.today

Table of Contents

REGIONAL CHILI RECIPES — 2

ALABAMA-STYLE CHILI	3
BOSTON CHILI	4
CALIFORNIA-STYLE CHILI	5
CARIBBEAN-STYLE CHILI	7
CHICAGO-STYLE CHILI	8
CINCINNATI-STYLE CHILI	9
DETROIT-STYLE CHILI	10
FLORIDIAN BEEF & BLACK BEAN CHILI	11
GEORGIA-STYLE CHILI	12
HAWAIIAN CHILI	13
ILLINOIS TAVERN-STYLE CHILI	14
INDIANA HOOSIER CHILI	15
KANSAS CITY CHILI	16
LOUISIANA CAJUN CHILI	17
MEMPHIS-STYLE CHILI	18
MEXICAN-STYLE CHILI	19
MICHIGAN CHILI	21
NEW MEXICO CHILE VERDE	22
NEW ORLEANS-STYLE CHILI	23
NEW YORK-STYLE CHILI	24
OKLAHOMA-STYLE CHILI	25
ROCKY MOUNTAINS CHILI	26
SAN ANTONIO CHILI	27
SANTA FE CHILI	28
SOUTHERN CHILI	29
SOUTHWESTERN-STYLE CHILI	30
SPRINGFIELD CHILI	31
ST. LOUIS-STYLE CHILI	32
TEX-MEX CHILI	33
TEXAS-STYLE CHILI	34
VERMONT MAPLE CHILI	35
WEST COAST TURKEY CHILI	36

SPECIALTY CHILI RECIPES — 38

BARLEY CHILI	39
BEEF & BEAN CHILI	40

BEER BRAT CHILI	**41**
BLACK BEAN & CHORIZO CHILI	**42**
CARNE ADOVADA	**43**
CHICKPEA CHILI	**45**
CHILI CON CARNE	**47**
CHILI MAC & CHEESE	**49**
CHIPOTLE PORK CHILI	**51**
CORN & BLACK BEAN CHILI	**52**
FIREHOUSE CHILI	**53**
FRITO PIE	**54**
LENTIL CHILI	**55**
LIME CHICKEN CHILI	**56**
MEATY MUSHROOM CHILI	**57**
PEPPERONI CHILI	**58**
QUINOA CHILI	**59**
SMOKEY PEANUT BUTTER CHILI	**61**
SPICED APPLE CHILI	**62**

Regional Chili Recipes

Alabama-style Chili

Prep Time: 10 minutes
Cooking Time: 2 hours & 10 minutes
Servings: 10

Ingredients

- 1 can pinto beans (16 ounce), rinsed & drained
- 2 pounds ground beef
- 1 onion, chopped
- 4 garlic cloves, minced
- 1 bottle dark beer (12 ounce)
- 2 cans tomato sauce (8 ounces each)
- 1 tablespoon Worcestershire sauce
- ½ cup canned beef broth, if needed
- 1 can green chilies (6 ounce), chopped
- 1 teaspoon ground cumin
- 2 tablespoons chili powder
- 1 teaspoon hot sauce
- 1 teaspoon paprika

Directions

1. Cook the ground beef with garlic and onion over moderate heat until meat crumbles are brown, stirring frequently.
2. Next, combine the meat mix with beans and other ingredients; bring the mix to a boil, over moderate heat. Let simmer until flavors are blended well, for an hour, on low heat. Feel free to add more of beef broth, if needed.

Boston Chili

Prep Time: 20 minutes
Cooking Time: 1 hour & 10 minutes
Servings: 08

Ingredients

- 3 red bell peppers
- ¼ cup jalapeno pepper, slices chopped
- 3 yellow bell peppers
- 5 garlic cloves, large, minced
- 3 tablespoons ground cumin
- 2 tablespoons ground coriander
- 3 tablespoons chili powder
- 1 cup red onion, chopped
- 3 tablespoons Mexican dried oregano
- Olive oil
- 3 cans chopped tomatoes with juice (16 ounces each)
- 2 cans black beans (16 ounces each), undrained
- 3 cans black beans (16 ounces each), drained & rinsed
- 2 cups strong brewed coffee
- Salt, to taste

Directions

1. Place the fresh yellow and red peppers on the grill; cook for a couple of minutes, until charred. Place them in a paper bag to sweat using a pair of tongs. Remove the peppers from bags and let cool then, remove the skins. Core & seed, then cut them into small, bite-sized pieces; set aside in a large bowl.
2. Next, over moderate heat in a large fry pan; toast the dried spices with a teaspoon of salt until fragrant, for a couple of minutes. Remove the pan from heat and immediately pour the toasted spices into a medium-sized bowl; set aside.
3. Now, pour olive oil (enough to cover the bottom of your pot) in a large 5-quart pot & heat the oil until hot. Add the chopped jalapeños and onions; cook until softened; add and cook the garlic for a couple of minutes, until the garlic is transparent, stirring frequently. Add the black beans and tomatoes, (along with any accumulated juices), and

the spice mixture; give it a good stir. Cover the pot; slightly decrease the heat & cook the mix for 15 minutes.
4. Meanwhile, brew the coffee and add after the 15 minutes; give it a good stir; continue to cook the chili for 10 minutes more. Taste & adjust the amount of seasonings, as needed. Remove from the heat; serve and enjoy.

California-style Chili

Prep Time: 20 minutes
Cooking Time: 3 hours & 20 minutes
Servings: 08

Ingredients

- 1 large onion, chopped
- 4 medium tomatoes, peeled & coarsely chopped
- 1 medium onion, chopped
- 1 ½ cups water
- 1 cup pitted black olives, coarsely chopped
- 2 stalks celery, chopped
- 1 tablespoon brown sugar
- ½ teaspoon each of pepper & salt
- 1 green pepper, seeded & chopped
- 2 garlic cloves, crushed
- 1-pound lean pork, cut into ¼" cubes
- 4 tablespoons bacon drippings or lard
- 1 cup Monterey jack cheese, shredded
- 2 pounds round steaks, trimmed; cut into ¼" cubes
- 1 tablespoon flour
- 5 tablespoons chili powder
- 1 tablespoon dried oregano
- 2 bay leaves
- 1 tablespoon red wine vinegar
- 1 tablespoon salt

Directions

1. Simmer the tomatoes with water, celery, 1 large onion, ½ teaspoon pepper and salt over moderate heat in a medium saucepan for half an hour, covered. Uncover and cook for 30 more minutes; set aside.
2. Meanwhile, over moderate heat in a large Dutch oven, sauté the medium onion, garlic, and green pepper in the lard for 3 to 5 minutes. Once done; remove the vegetables from the pan using a large, slotted spoon & set aside.
3. Add meats to the Dutch oven & cook for 5 to 8 minutes, until turn brown, over medium-high heat. Feel free to add more of lard, if needed. Add flour to the browned meats, giving it a good stir. Let simmer for a minute or two.
4. Return the vegetable mixture with the meats to the Dutch oven. Add the bay leaves, chili powder, 1 tablespoon salt, vinegar, brown sugar, and oregano. Add the tomato sauce; give it a good stir. Cover & let simmer for 2 hours, over low heat. Add more of water, if needed.
5. Add the cheese and olives; let simmer for 45 more minutes, covered, stirring often.
6. Remove the bay leaves.
7. Serve in individual bowls with a tossed salad and corn bread with more cheese and finely chopped onions, if desired.

Caribbean-style Chili

Prep Time: 20 minutes
Cooking Time: 35 minutes
Servings: 12

Ingredients

- 1 ½ pounds ground round
- 1 can cannellini beans (15 ounce)
- 1 ½ cups onion, chopped
- 2 garlic cloves, crushed
- 1 can black beans (15 ounce), drained
- 2 ½ cups yellow bell pepper, chopped
- 1 tablespoon ground cumin
- 2 teaspoons white sugar
- 1 can kidney beans (15 ounce), drained
- 2 cans stewed tomatoes (14.5 ounces each)
- 1 can tomato paste (6 ounce)
- 2 tablespoons balsamic vinegar
- 1 teaspoon olive oil
- ⅓ cup fresh cilantro, chopped
- 1 tablespoon hot paprika
- ¼ teaspoon ground cloves
- 1 tablespoon Chile powder
- ½ teaspoon salt

Directions

1. Cook the ground round over moderate heat in a large, deep skillet until evenly brown; drain well & set aside.
2. Coat a Dutch oven with the cooking spray & place it over moderate heat. Once hot, cook the garlic and onion in olive oil until onion turns tender. Next, add and cook the yellow pepper until tender. Season with Chile powder, cumin, sugar, paprika, cloves, and salt. Stir in the kidney beans, stewed tomatoes, cannellini beans, and black beans.
3. Pour in water (enough to cover) and bring it to a boil, over moderate heat. Stir in the tomato paste and meat; bring it to a boil again. Let simmer for half an hour.
4. Remove from the heat & stir in the vinegar. Serve hot; topped with fresh cilantro and enjoy.

Chicago-style Chili

Prep Time: 20 minutes
Cooking Time: 4 hours & 10 minutes
Servings: 10

Ingredients

- 4 cans kidney beans (14.5 ounces each)
- 1 bottle beer (12 fluid ounce)
- 4 cans diced tomatoes (15 ounces each)
- 6 garlic cloves, minced
- 1 bottle tomato-based chili sauce (12 ounce)
- ½ teaspoon garlic powder
- 2 pounds ground beef
- 1 large white onion, chopped
- 2 tablespoons chili seasoning
- ½ teaspoon onion powder
- 1 teaspoon black pepper
- ½ teaspoon cayenne pepper
- 1 teaspoon Worcestershire sauce
- ½ teaspoon oregano
- 1 teaspoon hot sauce
- ¼ cup sugar

Directions

1. Cook the ground beef over moderate heat in a large pot until evenly brown. Drain any excess fat off.
2. Next, mix in the diced tomatoes, onion, kidney beans, chili sauce, beer, garlic, cayenne pepper, chili seasoning, onion, garlic powder, black pepper, oregano, sugar, Worcestershire sauce, and hot sauce. Bring the mix to a boil, over moderate heat. Once done; decrease the heat to low, let simmer for 4 hours, stirring now and then.

Cincinnati-style Chili

Prep Time: 20 minutes
Cooking Time: 3 hours & 30 minutes
Servings: 10

Ingredients

- 2 pounds lean ground beef
- 1 can tomato sauce (15 ounce)
- 2 tablespoons vinegar
- ½ square unsweetened chocolate (1 ounce)
- 2 teaspoons Worcestershire sauce
- ¼ cup chili powder
- 1 teaspoon ground cumin
- 2 onions, finely chopped
- 1 teaspoon ground cinnamon
- 5 whole allspice berries
- ½ teaspoon ground cayenne pepper
- 4 garlic cloves, minced
- 1 bay leaf
- 5 whole cloves
- 1 quart water, or amount to cover
- 1 ½ teaspoons salt

Directions

1. Cover the ground beef with cold water in a large pan; bring it to a boil, over moderate heat, stirring & breaking up the meat to a fine texture using a fork.
2. Slowly boil the meat for half an hour, until thoroughly cooked.
3. Add onions followed by garlic, vinegar, tomato sauce, chocolate, and Worcestershire sauce. Stir in the chili powder, cinnamon, cumin, cayenne pepper, and salt until mixed well. Add allspice berries, bay leaf, and cloves.
4. Bring it to a boil. Once done; decrease the heat to a simmer & cook for 3 hours, stirring occasionally. Feel free to add more of water, if needed to prevent the chili from burning.

Detroit-style Chili

Prep Time: 10 minutes
Cooking Time: 1 hour & 10 minutes
Servings: 06

Ingredients

- ½ pound ground chuck
- ¼ teaspoon ground thyme
- 1 cup tomato sauce
- ¼ cup water
- 1 teaspoon chili powder
- ½ teaspoon garlic powder
- ¼ teaspoon dried oregano
- ½ teaspoon onion powder
- 1 teaspoon sugar
- ¼ teaspoon cumin
- 1 teaspoon salt

Directions

1. Brown the ground beef with onion, over moderate heat in a large saucepan until the meat is cooked through; drain well. Add black pepper and salt. Add tomato sauce & water; stir well
2. Add the spices & let simmer for an hour, for over low heat. Feel free to slowly add more of water, if needed to thin this sauce.
3. Serve on top of hot dogs or loose meat with diced onion and mustard.

Floridian Beef & Black Bean Chili

Prep Time: 10 minutes
Cooking Time: 1 hour & 20 minutes
Servings: 04

Ingredients

- 1 tablespoon freshly chopped herbs
- 1 ½ pound beef chuck, trimmed any excess fat & cut into 1" pieces
- 1 tablespoon brown sugar
- 2 teaspoons flour
- 1 yellow onion, diced
- 4 cloves garlic, minced
- 1 can black beans (15 ounces), drained & rinsed
- 1 can fire-roasted tomatoes (14.5 ounces)
- 2 teaspoons grainy mustard
- 1 lime
- ½ cup Greek yogurt
- 1 can beef stock (14.5 ounces)
- Chopped parsley or cilantro, for garnish
- 1 cup Guinness beer
- Cornbread, jarred jalapeños
- 2 tablespoons extra-virgin olive oil
- Pepper & salt to taste

Directions

1. Sprinkle the meat with the flour & a pinch of salt.
2. Next, over moderate heat in a large Dutch oven; heat a tablespoon of olive oil until hot. Work in batches, add the steak & sear on both sides, until browned. Once done, remove the steak from the pot; set aside.
3. Add oil to the pot & sauté onions until they begin to soften. Add the garlic & continue to sauté until the garlic is fragrant, for a minute. Add in the chopped herbs and brown sugar, sauté for a minute more.
4. Add tomatoes, beans, beer, and stock. Add steak to the pot, add a pinch of salt. Cover & let simmer for 3 hours, on medium low heat, stirring frequently and don't let it stick to the bottom.
5. Swirl in the two teaspoons of grainy mustard; give it a good stir.
6. Blend the yogurt with the lime juice.
7. Serve with a drizzle of the yogurt, chopped cilantro & cornbread.

Georgia-style Chili

Prep Time: 10 minutes
Cooking Time: 1 hour & 30 minutes
Servings: 06

Ingredients

- 1-pound lean ground beef
- 1 can tomatoes, crushed
- 3 tablespoons chili powder, divided
- 1 tablespoon shortening
- 2 cups tomato juice
- 1 onion, chopped
- 2 stalks celery, diced
- 1 can kidney bean
- Pepper & salt to taste
- 1 green pepper, diced

Directions

1. Season the ground beef with pepper and salt to taste.
2. Brown the onion and beef, mixed with 1 tablespoon of chili powder, in the shortening.
3. Next, add the tomato juice followed by green pepper, celery, and leftover chili powder.
4. Slowly simmer until vegetables are just tender, for 45 minutes.
5. Feel free to add more of water or tomato juice if mixture cooks down
6. Add tomatoes & let simmer for 15 more minutes; then add the kidney beans & let simmer for a couple of more minutes, until beans are just tender.

Hawaiian Chili

Prep Time: 20 minutes
Cooking Time: 30 minutes
Servings: 10

Ingredients

- 2 pounds ground beef
- 6 onions, chopped
- 2 red bell peppers, seeded and chopped
- 1 can tomato sauce (16 ounce)
- 2 tablespoons chili powder
- 2 cans stewed tomatoes (16 ounces each), with juice
- 1 can pineapple chunks (16 ounce), drained
- 2 cans kidney beans (15.5 ounces each), with liquid
- 2 teaspoons salt

Directions

1. Cook the ground beef over moderate heat in a large Dutch oven until barely pink, stirring constantly. As you cook the meat; don't forget to break it into small pieces. Stir in the bell pepper and onions, cook for 5 minutes, until the onions have turned translucent and softened, and the meat has browned. Transfer the meat into a large mesh strainer; pressing to expel any excess fat.
2. Place the meat into the Dutch oven again along with the kidney beans, stewed tomatoes, pineapple chunks, and tomato sauce, season with chili powder & salt. Bring the mix to a boil, over moderate heat. Once done; decrease the heat to medium-low & let simmer until chili reaches desired consistency, for 10 minutes, uncovered.

Illinois Tavern-style Chili

Prep Time: 20 minutes
Cooking Time: 2 hours & 20 minutes
Servings: 08

Ingredients

- 2 pounds ground beef
- 3 cloves garlic, minced
- 2 medium onions, chopped
- 3 teaspoons cumin
- 1 can chopped tomatoes with juice
- 3 tablespoons chili powder
- 4 cups kidney beans
- 3 tablespoons instant Masa corn flour
- 1 cup tomato sauce
- Cheddar cheese
- 1 can of beer
- Pepper & salt to taste

Directions

1. Cook the beef over moderate heat in a large pot until brown; drain the fat.
2. Add & mix in the leftover ingredients except cheddar cheese and Masa.
3. Let simmer for 2 hours, stirring now and then.
4. Stir in the Masa to thicken up. Serve immediately topped with the cheese. Enjoy.

Indiana Hoosier chili

Prep Time: 20 minutes
Cooking Time: 1 hour & 30 minutes
Servings: 12

Ingredients

- 3 tablespoons chili powder
- ½ cup green pepper, chopped
- 2 pounds lean ground beef (90% lean)
- ¾ cup celery, chopped
- 2 cups onions, chopped
- 1 tablespoon brown sugar
- 2 cans stewed tomatoes (14 ½ ounces each)
- 1 can tomato juice (46 ounces)
- 3 garlic cloves, minced
- ½ cup uncooked elbow macaroni
- 1 can condensed beef broth (10 ½ ounces), undiluted
- ¼ teaspoon pepper
- 1 can kidney beans (15 ounces), rinsed & drained
- ½ teaspoon salt

Directions

1. Cook the beef over moderate heat in a Dutch oven until no longer pink and turn brown. As you cook the meat; break it up into crumbles. Add the onion followed by celery, garlic, and green pepper. Continue to cook until the vegetables are just tender.
2. Add the leftover ingredients (except macaroni and beans); bring the mix to a boil. Decrease the heat; cover & let simmer for 1 ½ hours. During the last 30 minutes; add the macaroni & stir in the beans; cook until heated through.

Kansas City Chili

Prep Time: 20 minutes
Cooking Time: 8 hours & 10 minutes
Servings: 08

Ingredients

- 3 tablespoons light brown sugar
- 1 to 2 pounds boneless pork butt or pork shoulder; trimmed of fat & cut into 2" chunks
- 2 teaspoons granulated garlic
- 1 teaspoon. ground cumin
- 3 garlic cloves, finely chopped
- 1 jalapeño pepper, seeded & finely chopped
- 2 tablespoons hot sauce
- 1 large onion, diced
- 2 cans dark red kidney beans (15.5-ounce each), drained
- 1 small can tomato paste (6 ounces)
- 3 tablespoons chili powder
- ½ teaspoon chili flakes
- 2 tablespoons Worcestershire sauce
- 1 bottle pale ale-style beer (12-ounce)
- 3 cups chicken stock
- 1 can tomatoes (28-ounce), diced
- 2 tablespoons olive oil
- Freshly ground black pepper & kosher salt, to taste

For Garnish:
- Bacon
- ½ cup cheddar cheese
- Sliced scallions

Directions

1. Season the meat with pepper and salt, cumin & granulated garlic.
2. Placing the pork chunks into the bottom of your crock pot.
3. Add the leftover ingredients to the pot; give it a good stir & cook for 6 to 8 hours on low or for 3 hours on high.
4. Pull the chunks of pork apart using a pair of forks. Adjust the seasonings to your likings & garnish with the garnishing ingredients.

Louisiana Cajun Chili

Prep Time: 10 minutes
Cooking Time: 50 minutes
Servings: 06

Ingredients

- 1 can pinto beans (15 ounce), undrained
- 2 pounds ground beef
- 1 cup onion, chopped
- 2 garlic cloves, minced
- 1 can diced tomatoes (14 ½ ounce), undrained
- 1 cup green pepper, chopped
- 1 can tomato sauce (8 ounce)
- 1 tablespoon honey
- 2 tablespoons chili powder
- 1 teaspoon dried oregano
- 1 teaspoon dried parsley flakes
- 1 -2 teaspoon Cajun seasoning
- 1 teaspoon ground cumin

Directions

1. Over moderate heat in a Dutch oven, cook the meat with onion, garlic, and green pepper.
2. In the meantime, process the beans with liquid in a blender until smooth.
3. Drain the fat from Dutch oven; add the beans & leftover ingredients.
4. Let simmer for 35 to 40 minutes, uncovered.

Memphis-style Chili

Prep Time: 20 minutes
Cooking Time: 2 hours & 40 minutes
Servings: 08

Ingredients

- 2 tablespoons canola oil
- 2 cups yellow onion, chopped
- 1 boneless pork shoulder roast (2-pound), cut into 1" cubes
- 2 teaspoons garlic powder
- 1 tablespoon chili powder
- 2 teaspoons dry mustard
- 1 tablespoon paprika
- 3 cups chicken stock
- ½ teaspoon cayenne pepper
- 2 cups barbecue sauce
- 1 can baked beans (15-ounce)
- 2 cans navy beans (15-ounces each), drained and rinsed
- 1 teaspoon celery salt
- 2 teaspoons dried oregano
- Toppings: shredded Cheddar cheese, sour cream, sliced cabbage
- Fritos corn chips, to serve

Directions

1. Over moderate heat in a large Dutch oven; heat 1 tablespoon of oil until hot. Add & cook half of the cubed pork roast for 7 to 9 minutes, until browned on all sides. Transfer to a large plate. Drain the oil from your Dutch oven. Repeat with the leftover pork and oil.
2. Add onion to the Dutch oven. Cook for 8 to 10 minutes, until caramelized slightly, stirring occasionally. Add the browned pork followed by garlic powder, chili powder, paprika, oregano, celery salt, mustard, and cayenne; cook for a minute, until fragrant, stirring constantly. Add the barbecue sauce, stock, baked beans, and navy beans; bring the mix to a boil, over moderate heat.
3. Decrease the heat to low; cover & let simmer for 1 hour and 30 minutes, until the meat is very tender.
4. Increase the heat to medium-high; let simmer for 20 minutes, until thickened slightly, uncovered, stirring occasionally. Serve with chips.

Mexican-style Chili

Prep Time: 20 minutes
Cooking Time: 30 minutes
Servings: 04

Ingredients

- 1 teaspoon dried Mexican oregano
- 2 pounds lean ground beef, preferably organic
- 1 tablespoon canola oil
- 3 garlic cloves, minced
- 1 medium yellow onion, chopped
- 2 tablespoons chili powder
- 1 teaspoon ground cumin
- ½ cup enchilada sauce
- 1 can no-salt-added kidney beans (15-ounce), rinsed & drained
- ¼ teaspoon cayenne pepper
- 1 tablespoon Mexican chili paste (store-bought or homemade)
- 2 cans diced tomatoes (15-ounces each), in juice
- 1 can no-salt-added pinto beans (15-ounce), rinsed & drained
- 3 tablespoons unsweetened chopped chocolate
- 1 teaspoon kosher salt

Optional Toppings:
- Cotija cheese, crumbled
- Crema
- Tortilla strips
- Lime wedges
- Chopped cilantro

Directions

1. Over moderate heat in a large pot; heat the oil until hot. Add the onions & cook for 5 minutes, until translucent, stirring occasionally. Stir in the garlic & cook for 2 to 3 minutes, until golden slightly, stirring occasionally.
2. Add the beef; breaking it up using a large wooden spoon & cook for 5 minutes. Once done; add the cumin, chili powder, oregano, chili paste, cayenne and salt; give it a good stir until the beef is coated with the seasonings.
3. Next, add the tomatoes along with any accumulated juices, beans, chocolate, and enchilada sauce; give it a good stir. Decrease the heat; cover & let simmer for 30 minutes, until thickened, stirring occasionally.
4. Garnish with toppings of your choice; serve and enjoy.

Michigan Chili

Prep Time: 20 minutes
Cooking Time: 2 hours & 10 minutes
Servings: 10

Ingredients

- ½ cup thinly sliced pork or 3 slices bacon, cooked & chopped
- Michigan ski country chili mix
- 1 ½ pounds ground chuck
- 1 can tomatoes (14.5 ounce), diced
- 2 tablespoons brown sugar
- 1 cup red wine
- 2 cups beef broth (16 ounces)
- 1 tablespoon oil
- Pepper & salt to taste

Directions

For Beans:
1. Pick through the beans and remove the shriveled, discolored beans and any foreign material, rinse well.
2. Next, place the beans with approximately 8 cups of water in a large bowl. Soak at room temperature for 4 hours
3. Drain the beans & place in a 4-quart pot with 8 cups water.
4. Bring it to a boil, over moderate heat. Once done; decrease the heat & let simmer for 45 minutes, covered.
5. Remove from the heat; drain & set aside until needed.

For Soup:
1. Over moderate heat in a 4-quart pot; heat the oil until hot. Cut the bacon into smaller pieces & carefully sauté in hot oil.
2. Add the ground beef into pot & continue to cook.
3. Stir in the brown sugar and contents of chili pix packet.
4. Add the drained, cooked beans followed by tomatoes, wine, and broth to the pot.
5. Bring it to a boil, over moderate heat. Decrease the heat & let simmer for an hour, covered.
6. Remove the Chile peppers then, sprinkle with pepper and salt to taste.
7. Serve immediately; topped with sour cream, tortilla chips or grated cheddar cheese. Enjoy.

New Mexico Chile Verde

Prep Time: 30 minutes
Cooking Time: 3 hours & 30 minutes
Servings: 06

Ingredients

- 4 pounds pork butt, trimmed & cut into 1 ½" cubes
- ¼ cup oil
- 2 large onions, peeled & chopped
- 1 tablespoon ground cumin
- 4 garlic cloves, minced
- 1 tablespoon oregano
- 2 Hatch peppers, chopped
- 1 tablespoon ground coriander
- 2 Poblano peppers, chopped
- 1-pound tomatillos; peeled, cleaned, and chopped
- 2 bay leaves
- 4 cups chicken stock or water
- 1-2 jalapeno peppers, seeded & diced
- 3 tablespoons corn flour (masa)
- A bunch of cilantro (large), chopped
- 1 tablespoon salt, divided
- Lime wedges for garnish

Directions

1. Over moderate heat in a large pot; heat the oil until hot. Add the pork with 2 teaspoons of salt. Cook the pork until all sides turn brown, stirring now and then. Remove the pork from pot & pour out all rendered fat, reserving approximately 1 tablespoon.
2. Add onions, oregano, coriander, cumin, and salt to the pot. Sauté for 3 to 5 minutes. Once done; add the peppers and garlic; sauté for 3 to 5 more minutes. Add the chopped tomatillos, cilantro, and bay leaves. Toss the pork with masa & add it to the pot again; give it a good stir.
3. Lastly add the water. Bring the mix to a boil, over moderate heat. Once done; decrease the heat to low. Cover & let simmer until the pork is falling apart, for 3 hours, stirring now and then.
4. Break the pork up even more using a pair of forks. Sprinkle with pepper and salt to taste. Enjoy.

New Orleans-style Chili

Prep Time: 20 minutes
Cooking Time: 1 hour & 20 minutes
Servings: 06

Ingredients

- 1 cup green pepper, chopped
- 2 pounds ground beef
- 1 can pinto beans (15 ounce), undrained
- 2 garlic cloves, minced
- 1 cup onion, chopped
- 1 teaspoon dried parsley flakes
- 1 can diced tomatoes (14 ½ ounce), undrained
- 2 tablespoons chili powder
- 1 tablespoon honey
- 1 can tomato sauce (8 ounce)
- 1 teaspoon ground cumin
- 1 -2 teaspoon Cajun seasoning
- 1 teaspoon dried oregano

Directions

1. Over moderate heat in a large, Dutch oven; brown the meat with onion, garlic, and green pepper.
2. In the meantime, process the beans with liquid in a blender until completely smooth.
3. Drain the fat from Dutch oven; add the beans & leftover ingredients.
4. Let simmer for 35 to 40 minutes, uncovered.

New York-style Chili

Prep Time: 10 minutes
Cooking Time: 50 minutes
Servings: 10

Ingredients

- 2 medium onions, chopped
- 2 pounds ground beef
- 1 can tomato paste, approximately 6 oz
- 2 teaspoons Worcestershire sauce
- ¼ teaspoon cinnamon
- 2 teaspoons vinegar
- 2 tablespoons chili powder
- 1 garlic clove, minced
- 3 cups water
- 1 tablespoon black pepper
- 2 teaspoons salt

Directions

1. Brown the onions and beef over moderate heat in a large skillet or heavy pot.
2. Work in batches & place a portion in the blender container, blend for a couple of seconds.
3. Mix the meat mixture with vinegar, tomato paste, cinnamon, water, Worcestershire, chili powder, salt, pepper, and garlic.
4. Let simmer until thick, for an hour or two. Serve on top of spaghetti or hot dogs. Enjoy.

Oklahoma-style Chili

Prep Time: 20 minutes
Cooking Time: 1 hour & 20 minutes
Servings: 08

Ingredients

- 24 ounces tomato sauce
- 2 pounds ground beef
- 29 ounces tomatoes in juice, diced
- 2 tablespoons masa
- 1 yellow onion, chopped
- 2 tablespoons chili powder
- 1 teaspoon Worcestershire sauce
- 2 teaspoons cumin
- 1 tablespoon garlic powder
- ½ teaspoon cayenne pepper
- 2 teaspoons each of coarse ground black pepper, and kosher salt

Directions

1. In a large pot, combine the ground beef with garlic powder.
2. Cook until browned, over moderate heat. Drain any excess fat off, and then, mix in the leftover ingredients.
3. Stir well; cover & decrease the heat to low. Let simmer for an hour, stirring now and then.
4. Serve with the sour cream, chopped onions, shredded cheddar cheese, corn bread and Fritos.

Rocky Mountains Chili

Prep Time: 20 minutes
Cooking Time: 3 hours & 10 minutes
Servings: 08

Ingredients

- 2 pounds ground beef or elk, or deer
- 1 can tomatoes (16 ounce), broken up
- 4 ounces diced green chilies
- 2 pickled jalapeno peppers, chopped
- 4 tablespoons tomato paste
- 2 medium yellow onions, chopped
- 3 tablespoons chili powder
- 1 tablespoon oregano
- 2 cans beef broth (14 ½ ounces each)
- 1 can pinto beans (15 ounce)
- 5 cups water
- 2 garlic cloves, minced
- 1 teaspoon ground cumin
- Oil, as needed
- 1 teaspoon salt

Directions

1. Brown the mean with garlic and onions in a bit of oil. Add tomatoes followed by jalapenos, chilies, tomato paste, seasonings, water, and beef broth. Bring the mix to a boil, over moderate heat.
2. Once done; decrease the heat to low & cook for 4 to 5 hours, stirring now and then. Adjust the amount of seasonings, if needed. During the last 30 minutes of cooking; add the beans. Serve hot in individual bowls with an assortment of condiments such as sliced olives, grated cheeses, chopped onions, Pico de Gallo, and so on.

San Antonio Chili

Prep Time: 10 minutes
Cooking Time: 2 hours & 20 minutes
Servings: 06

Ingredients

- 1 pound each of trimmed boneless stewing beef and stewing pork, cut into ½" cubes & patted dry
- 2 each ancho & guajillo chiles, 2 reconstituted
- ½ cup fresh cilantro leaves & tender stems
- 2 onions, thinly sliced
- Crumbled Mexican Cheese, as needed
- 6 garlic cloves, minced
- 1 tablespoon each of dried Mexican oregano and ground cumin
- 6 green onions (green and white parts only), very thinly sliced
- 1 jalapeño pepper or serrano, thinly sliced
- 2 tablespoons oil or lard
- Freshly ground black pepper & salt to taste

Directions

1. Transfer the reconstituted chilies with liquid to a blender. Add the cilantro & purée until completely smooth; set the puree aside.
2. In the meantime, over moderate heat in a large, Dutch oven; heat the lard until melted. Work in batches; add pork and beef; cook for 2 minutes, until all sides turn brown. Transfer to a large plate; set aside. Decrease the heat to medium.
3. Preheat your oven to 325 F. Add sliced onions to the pan & cook for 4 minutes, until softened, stirring. Add garlic, oregano, and cumin; cook for a minute, stirring frequently. Return the pork and beef to the pan. Add the kept-aside ancho & guajillo chili mixture; give it a good stir. Season with black pepper and salt to taste. Bring the mix to a boil, over moderate heat. Cover & transfer to your preheated oven. Bake for 2 hours, until the meat is very tender.
4. Ladle into individual, warm soup plates and then, garnish with Serrano pepper & green onions then, sprinkle with the cheese.

Santa Fe Chili

Prep Time: 20 minutes
Cooking Time: 4 hours & 10 minutes
Servings: 16

Ingredients

- 2 cans kidney beans (16 ounces each), rinsed & drained
- 2 pounds ground beef
- 1 medium onion, chopped
- 2 cans black beans (15 ounces each), rinsed & drained
- 1 can diced tomatoes & green chilies (10 ounces)
- 2 envelopes ranch salad dressing mix
- 2 cans pinto beans (15 ounces each), rinsed & drained
- 1 can diced tomatoes (14 ½ ounces), undrained
- 3 cans white corn (7 ounces each), drained
- 1 can V8 juice (11 ½ ounces)
- 2 envelopes taco seasoning

Optional Ingredients:
- Sour cream, corn chips and shredded cheddar cheese

Directions

1. Over moderate heat in a large skillet; cook the onion and beef until meat is no longer pink, for a couple of minutes; drain well. Transfer to a 6-qt. slow cooker and then, immediately stir in the corn, beans, tomatoes, juice, taco seasoning and salad dressing mix.
2. Cover & cook until heated through, for 4 to 6 hours on high. Serve with sour cream, corn chips and cheese. Enjoy.

Southern Chili

Prep Time: 10 minutes
Cooking Time: 4 hours & 20 minutes
Servings: 08

Ingredients

- 16-ounce canned red kidney beans, rinsed & drained
- 1 ½ pounds lean ground beef
- 14 ½ ounce canned tomatoes, diced
- 1 small green bell pepper, chopped
- 2 garlic cloves, minced
- 1 medium onion, chopped
- 2 cups beef broth
- 1 teaspoon each of ground cumin, pepper & salt
- 1 ½ tablespoons chili powder

Directions

1. Over moderate heat in a large skillet; cook the onion with ground beef, garlic, and bell pepper; cook & stir until beef is no longer pink and crumbles. Once cooked, drain the mixture well.
2. Place the cooked mixture in a 5-quart slow cooker and immediately stir in the beans, diced tomatoes, broth, pepper, chili powder, ground cumin, and salt. Cook for 5 to 6 hours at low or for 3 to 4 hours at high. To thicken consistency, immediately stir in the finely crushed saltine crackers. Serve and enjoy.

Southwestern-style Chili

Prep Time: 20 minutes
Cooking Time: 10 hours & 10 minutes
Servings: 08

Ingredients

- 1 white onion, chopped
- 1 pound ground beef
- 1 can sweet corn, drained
- ¼ cup chili powder
- 1 green pepper, chopped
- 1 tablespoon cumin
- 1 can green chilies, drained
- 1 garlic clove, minced
- 1 can kidney beans, drained
- ½ teaspoon garlic powder
- 1 teaspoon fresh ground pepper
- 1 can black beans, drained
- 3 jars of Pace Salsa mild (10 ounces each)

For Toppings, Optional:
- sour cream
- Cheddar cheese, freshly grated
- green onions

Directions

1. Add onion with ground beef, garlic powder, garlic clove, green pepper, cumin, chili powder, pepper, salsa, kidney beans, black beans, chilies, and corn into the Crockpot.
2. Cook for 8 to 10 hours on low heat
3. Serve with your favorite toppings such as rice, cornbread, crackers, and/or noodles.

Springfield Chili

Prep Time: 20 minutes
Cooking Time: 1 hour & 10 minutes
Servings: 06

Ingredients

- 1 pound turkey breast, coarsely ground
- 2 ¼ cups onions, finely chopped, divided
- 1 slice bacon, finely chopped
- 2 garlic cloves, minced
- 1 teaspoon Worcestershire sauce
- ½ pound sirloin, coarsely ground
- 1 can beer (12 ounce)
- 3 tablespoons chili powder
- 1 can diced tomatoes (14 ½ ounce), undrained
- ¼ teaspoon ground cumin
- 1 can tomato sauce (8 ounce), without added salt
- ½ cup reduced-fat cheddar cheese, shredded
- 1 can pinto beans (15 ounce), rinsed & drained
- ½ teaspoon kosher salt
- oyster crackers (optional)

Directions

1. Over moderate heat in a large Dutch oven; cook the bacon until browned, for 5 minutes. Stir in 2 cups of onion; cover & cook for 5 minutes, until onion is tender. Uncover & immediately stir in the garlic; cook for a minute more.
2. Increase the heat to medium-high; add the sirloin and turkey to the pan. Cook until browned, for 5 minutes, stirring to crumble. Add the beer; cook for 7 minutes, until the liquid is decreased to approximately ⅓ cup.
3. Stir in the chili powder and Worcestershire sauce with kosher salt, ground cumin, diced tomatoes, and tomato sauce. Cover and decrease the heat & let simmer until the mixture thickens, for 30 minutes. Stir in the beans; cook until heated thoroughly, for 10 minutes.
4. Ladle a cup of chili into each of 6 bowls and top each with approximately 4 teaspoons of cheese & 2 teaspoons of onion. Serve with the crackers and enjoy.

St. Louis-style Chili

Prep Time: 20 minutes
Cooking Time: 2 hours & 10 minutes
Servings: 10

Ingredients

- 1 large onion, chopped
- 2 pounds coarsely ground beef 85% lean
- 1 can pinto beans (16- ounce); drained & rinsed
- ¾ teaspoon sugar
- 2 cans whole tomatoes (16- ounce each) undrained, chopped
- 1 can tomato paste (6- ounce)
- 3 garlic cloves, crushed
- ½ teaspoon vinegar
- 2 tablespoons good quality chili powder
- ½ teaspoon ground cumin
- 1 small bay leaf
- 2 whole cloves
- 1 teaspoon salt
- 2 tablespoons oil
- ⅛ teaspoon ground red pepper

Directions

1. Over moderate heat in a large pot; heat the oil until hot. Sauté the garlic and onion until brown lightly. Add the ground beef & cook until browned. Drain any excess fat off.
2. Add the leftover ingredients. Let simmer for an hour, uncovered. Remove the cloves and bay leaf. Top with the chopped green onions and grated yellow cheese. Serve and enjoy

Tex-Mex Chili

Prep Time: 20 minutes
Cooking Time: 6 hours & 20 minutes
Servings: 12

Ingredients

- 3 pounds beef stew meat
- 1 teaspoon chili powder
- 3 garlic cloves, minced
- 1 can diced tomatoes (14 ½ ounces), undrained
- 3 cans kidney beans (16 ounces each), rinsed & drained
- 1 can tomato paste (6 ounces)
- 3 cans tomato sauce (15 ounces each)
- 1 cup water
- ¾ cup salsa verde
- 1 envelope chili seasoning
- ½ teaspoon ground cumin
- 2 teaspoons dried minced onion
- ½ teaspoon crushed red pepper flakes
- 1 tablespoon canola oil
- ½ teaspoon cayenne pepper

Optional Ingredients:
- Minced fresh cilantro
- Shredded cheddar cheese
- Additional salsa verde
- Sour cream
- Fresno peppers
- Sliced jalapeno

Directions

1. Over moderate heat in a large skillet; cook beef until browned. Once done; immediately add the garlic & cook for a minute more. Transfer to a 6 qt. slow cooker.
2. Once done; stir in the tomato paste, tomatoes, tomato sauce, beans, water, seasonings, and salsa verde.
3. Cover & cook until meat is tender, for 6 to 8 hours on low.
4. Garnish each serving with your favorite toppings, as needed.

Texas-style Chili

Prep Time: 35 minutes
Cooking Time: 50 minutes
Servings: 08

Ingredients

- 2 pounds ground beef, (90% lean)
- 1 large onion, chopped
- 1 jalapeño pepper, ribs and seeds removed, chopped
- 4 garlic cloves, minced
- 1 green bell pepper, chopped
- 1 tablespoon paprika
- 1 tablespoon ground cumin
- 2 tablespoons chili powder
- 1 can tomato sauce (8 ounce)
- 1 can diced tomatoes & green chilies (10 ounce), undrained
- ½ cup low-fat sharp cheddar cheese (2 ounce), shredded
- 1 cup beer
- 1 teaspoon dried oregano
- 1 tablespoon vegetable oil
- ½ teaspoon each of freshly ground black pepper, and kosher salt

Optional Toppings:
- Shredded cheddar cheese
- Sliced green onions
- Sour cream

Directions

1. Over moderate heat in a large Dutch oven; heat the oil until hot. Once done; decrease the heat; add the onion with jalapeño pepper and bell pepper; cook for 5 to 7 minutes, until tender, stirring occasionally. Add and cook the garlic for a minute more.
2. Add the beef & cook for 7 to 10 minutes, breaking the beef into small crumbles, stirring now and then. Pour any dripping off, as needed.
3. Add paprika, chili powder, oregano, cumin, black pepper & salt.
4. Add the tomato sauce, green chilies & diced tomatoes, and beer; bring the mix to a boil. Decrease the heat to low; cover & cook for half an hour. Add the shredded cheese. Serve with toppings of your choice.

Vermont Maple Chili

Prep Time: 10 minutes
Cooking Time: 1 hour & 20 minutes
Servings: 06

Ingredients

- 4 cups canned kidney beans, drained
- 1 pound kidney beans or dried cranberry beans
- 2 garlic cloves, minced
- 1 cup onions, chopped
- 2 pounds ground chuck
- 1 ½ teaspoons black pepper
- 15-ounces can tomato sauce
- 1 teaspoon ground allspice
- ½ slices sharp Cheddar cheese (2x2x¼" thick)
- 2 tablespoons vegetable oil
- ½ cup pure maple syrup
- 3 tablespoons chili powder
- 1 ½ teaspoons salt

Directions

1. Soak the beans in cold water for overnight; discard any stones and bad beans. Rinse the beans & place with fresh water in a large pot. Cook until tender, for an hour. Drain & reserve 4 cups of the beans.
2. Next, over moderate heat in a large, Dutch oven; sauté the garlic and onion in hot oil until soft. Add the meat, stirring now and then to keep it loose & crumbly; continue to cook until browned. Drain & discard any fat.
3. Add pepper, allspice, chili powder, maple syrup, tomato sauce, 2 cups water and salt. Bring the mix to a boil, over moderate heat. Decrease the heat to a low simmer & cook for 30 minutes, partially covered. Add the kept-aside beans & cook for more 15 minutes.
4. Cut the stars from the cheese slices using a cookie cutter. To serve, spoon the chili into individual bowls & top each with 2 to 3 stars.

West Coast Turkey Chili

Prep Time: 20 minutes
Cooking Time: 30 minutes
Servings: 06

Ingredients

- 3 cups turkey meat; cooked, cut in ½" cubes or substitute cooked chicken meat
- 1 cup green bell peppers, diced
- 2 garlic cloves, minced
- 1 ¼ cups onions, diced
- 3 tablespoons vegetable oil
- 1 cup red wine
- 28 ounces tomatoes, stewed, canned
- 1 tablespoon chili powder
- 19 ounces kidney beans, canned; drained and rinsed
- 1 teaspoon red pepper flakes, crushed
- ½ teaspoon cumin, freshly crushed
- 1 tablespoon fresh cilantro, chopped
- ½ teaspoon salt

Directions

1. Over moderate heat in a heavy bottom saucepan; heat the vegetable oil until hot. Add the onions followed by garlic, and green bell pepper; sauté until green bell pepper is tender-crisp and onions are translucent, for 5 minutes.
2. Add the tomatoes, kidney beans, turkey, wine, red pepper, cilantro, chili powder, salt, and cumin.
3. Increase the heat; bring the mix to a boil. Once done; immediately decrease the heat to low & let simmer for 25 minutes, uncovered.
4. Just before serving, garnish your dish with freshly chopped cilantro and enjoy.

Specialty Chili Recipes

Barley Chili

Prep Time: 20 minutes
Cooking Time: 1 hour & 10 minutes
Servings: 06

Ingredients

- ½ pound 90% lean ground beef
- 1 small onion, chopped
- ⅓ cup medium pearl barley
- 2 tablespoons all-purpose flour
- ¾ teaspoon ground cumin
- 1 ½ teaspoons beef bouillon granules
- ½ cup tomato sauce
- 1 teaspoon chili powder
- ¼ teaspoon dried oregano
- 4 cups water
- ¼ teaspoon salt

Directions

1. Over moderate heat in a large saucepan; cook the onion and beef until the meat is no longer pink; drain well. Stir in the flour and add the leftover ingredients; bring the mix to a boil.
2. Once done; decrease the heat & let simmer until barley is tender, for 1 hour, uncovered.

Beef & Bean Chili

Prep Time: 10 minutes
Cooking Time: 1 hour & 20 minutes
Servings: 06

Ingredients

- 2 large red onions, chopped
- 1 teaspoon sweet paprika
- 8 garlic cloves, chopped
- 1 can beef broth (14-ounce)
- 2 ⅓ pounds ground beef (approximately 15% fat)
- ¼ cup chili powder
- 2 tablespoons ground cumin
- 1 can diced tomatoes in juice (28-ounce)
- 2 cans kidney beans (15 ¼ ounces each), drained
- 1 tablespoon olive oil
- 5 tablespoons jalapeño chilies with seeds, chopped
- Sour cream
- Cheddar cheese, grated
- Green onions, chopped
- Fresh cilantro, chopped

Directions

1. Over moderate heat in a large, heavy pot; heat the oil until hot. Add the onions & sauté for 6 minutes, until brown.
2. Add garlic and jalapeños, sauté for a minute.
3. Add beef & sauté until brown, for 5 minutes. As you cook the meat; don't forget to break it up using the back of a fork.
4. Add the chili powder, paprika, and cumin, then mix in the tomatoes with juices, broth, and beans; bring the mix to a boil, over moderate heat.
5. Decrease the heat & let simmer until flavors blend and chili thickens, for 45 minutes, stirring occasionally. Skim any fat from the surface of chili. Let slightly cool.
6. Ladle chili into bowls. Serve immediately; topped with sour cream, grated cheese, cilantro, and green onions.

Beer Brat Chili

Prep Time: 10 minutes
Cooking Time: 5 hours & 10 minutes
Servings: 08

Ingredients

- 1 can Southwest or seasoned recipe black beans (15 ounces), undrained
- 1 can cannellini beans (15 ounces), rinsed & drained
- 1 medium sweet red pepper, chopped
- 1 can pinto beans (15 ounces), rinsed & drained
- 1 package fully cooked beer bratwurst links (14 ounces), sliced
- 1 ½ cups corn, frozen
- 1 can Italian diced tomatoes (14 ½ ounces), undrained
- 1 medium onion, finely chopped
- ¼ cup chili seasoning mix
- 1 garlic clove, minced
- 1 can diced tomatoes & green chilies (10 ounces), undrained

Directions

1. Combine all the ingredients together in a 5-qt. slow cooker. Cover & cook for 5 to 6 hours on low. Serve and enjoy.

Black Bean & Chorizo Chili

Prep Time: 20 minutes
Cooking Time: 50 minutes
Servings: 04

Ingredients

- 1 onion, chopped
- ½ pound ground Mexican chorizo, casing removed
- 16 ounces can kidney beans, drained
- 1 pound ground beef
- 3 garlic cloves, minced
- 1 green bell pepper, chopped
- 16 ounces can black beans, drained
- 1 tablespoon dried oregano
- 16 ounces can diced tomatoes (fire-roasted)
- 1 tablespoon chili powder
- 16 ounces can tomato sauce
- 1 teaspoon cumin
- 2 hot chilies, minced (jalapeno, Serrano, etc.)
- 1 teaspoon coriander
- ¼ can good beer
- 1 tablespoon cooking oil
- ¼ teaspoon salt
- cilantro, for garnish

Directions

1. Over moderate heat in a large frying pan; heat the oil until hot and then, brown the beef, onion, and chorizo for 3 to 5 minutes, stirring occasionally. Let the meat and onions to brown on one side. Break any large clumps of ground meat apart.
2. Add the onions and meat along with the leftover ingredients to a heavy-bottomed pot.
3. Pour the beer just enough to cover the ingredients with liquid.
4. Cover the pot & let simmer for 45 minutes, over low heat. Serve immediately, garnished with freshly chopped cilantro.

Carne Adovada

Prep Time: 10 minutes
Cooking Time: 3 hours & 20 minutes
Servings: 08

Ingredients

- 3 pounds boneless pork shoulder, trimmed and cut into 2-inch-thick cubes
- 4 whole dried ancho chilies, seeds & stems removed
- 1 quart (32 ounces) homemade or store-bought low-sodium chicken stock
- 2 tablespoons Asian fish sauce
- 4 whole dried pasilla chilies, seeds & stems removed
- 2 medium onions, thinly sliced (about 2 cups)
- 1 cup frozen orange juice concentrate
- 3 whole chipotle chilies canned in adobo
- ½ cup raisins
- 2 tablespoons white vinegar
- 6 medium cloves garlic, minced (about 2 tablespoons)
- 2 teaspoons dried oregano
- 1 tablespoon ground cumin
- 3 bay leaves
- 2 tablespoons vegetable oil
- Kosher salt

Optional Ingredients, For Serving:
- Cilantro
- Queso fresco
- Corn tortillas
- Lime wedges
- Diced onions

Directions

1. Add the dried chilies to large, heavy-bottomed stock pot or Dutch oven; cook for 2 to 5 minutes, until darkened slightly with intense, roasted aroma, over moderate heat, stirring frequently. Don't let it smoke. Add the chicken stock followed by chipotles in adobo, orange juice concentrate, raisins, fish sauce, and white vinegar. Bring the mix to a boil. Once done; decrease the heat to a bare simmer & let cook for 15 minutes, until chilies are completely softened. Blend into a smooth puree using an immersion blender; set aside.
2. Carefully pat pork cubes dry using a clean kitchen towel or paper towels. Next, over moderate heat in a large, heavy-bottomed Dutch oven; heat the vegetable oil until smoking. Add the pork & evenly spread over the bottom surface. Cook for 8 minutes, until bottom surface is browned well, undisturbed. Transfer the pork to a cutting board & set aside. Add garlic and onions to the Dutch oven & cook for 10 minutes, until softened & starting to brown, stirring frequently. Add cumin and oregano; cook for half a minute, until fragrant, stirring constantly.
3. Add chili mix to the Dutch oven; stir and scrape up any browned bits from the bottom. Once done; add the bay leaves along with the pork & any accumulated juices. Bring the mix to a boil. Once done; decrease the heat to a bare simmer. Cover & cook for 2 hours, until pork chunks break, leaving lid slightly ajar, stirring occasionally.
4. Season with salt to taste. Serve the pork with diced onions, cilantro, corn tortillas, queso fresco, and lime wedges.

Chickpea Chili

Prep Time: 10 minutes
Cooking Time: 1 hour & 20 minutes
Servings: 06

Ingredients

- 1-pound organic, grass-fed ground beef (93/7 fat ratio) or ground lamb
- 2 teaspoons ground cumin
- ½ teaspoon black pepper
- 1 teaspoon ground coriander
- ½ teaspoon ground ginger
- 1 teaspoon ground cinnamon
- ¼ teaspoon cayenne pepper or to taste
- 1 large onion, diced
- 6 large cloves garlic, pressed through garlic press
- 1 bay leaf
- ¼ teaspoon allspice
- 2 cups beef stock
- 1 teaspoon orange zest, slightly heaping
- 3 tablespoons tomato paste
- ¾ pound Campari tomatoes, chopped
- 2 large cans organic chickpeas (29 ounces each), drained
- ¼ cup orange juice, fresh
- 3 tablespoons cilantro, chopped
- Olive oil
- 1 ½ teaspoons fresh oregano leaves, chopped
- Salt to taste
- 2 tablespoons parsley, chopped
- Warm flatbread, to serve alongside

Directions

1. Prepare your spice mixture by mixing the cumin with ginger, black pepper, cinnamon, coriander, cayenne, and allspice in a small ramekin using a fork. Set aside.
2. Place a deep, heavy bottom pan or large pot or Dutch oven over moderate heat & drizzle in approximately 3 tablespoons of olive oil. Once hot, immediately add the diced onion & sauté until it just starts to soften, for 3 minutes.
3. Add in the ground beef or lamb & break up the meat into a fine crumble using a wooden spatula or spoon. Add a generous pinch or two of salt, plus spice mixture from the ramekin; cook the meat until mostly cooked through, for 3 to 5 minutes.
4. Next, add in the garlic, orange zest and bay leaf; stir to incorporate into the meat mixture until aromatic. Stir in the tomato paste.
5. Once done, add in the drained chickpeas; give it a good stir to mix and then, add the chopped tomatoes. Add in the beef stock and orange juice; stir to incorporate.
6. Bring the chickpea chili to a vigorous simmer, then decrease the heat; let simmer gently & bubble for 45 minutes, uncovered, stirring occasionally.
7. Once done, cover the chickpea chili & cook until the chickpeas are tender and thickened, for half an hour
8. To finish the chickpea chili, drizzle in approximately 2 to 3 tablespoons of olive oil to enrich it and add body to it then stir in the parsley, cilantro, and oregano. Serve hot with the warm flatbread on the side. Enjoy

Chili Con Carne

Prep Time: 30 minutes
Cooking Time: 1 hour & 10 minutes
Servings: 04

Ingredients

- 1 large onion
- 2 garlic cloves
- 1 heaped teaspoon hot chili powder
- 1 ¼ pounds lean minced beef
- 1 teaspoon paprika
- 400g can chopped tomatoes
- 1 teaspoon ground cumin
- 410g can red kidney beans
- 1 beef stock cube
- ½ teaspoon dried marjoram
- 1 red pepper
- 1 teaspoon sugar
- 2 tablespoons tomato purée
- 1 tablespoon oil

To Serve:
- Soured cream
- Plain boiled long grain rice

Directions

1. Chop 1 large onion into small dice. Cut 1 red pepper lengthways into half, remove the stalk & wash the seeds away, then chop. Peel & finely chop 2 cloves of garlic.
2. Over moderate heat in a large pan; heat 1 tablespoon of oil until hot.
3. Add and cook the onion; cook for 5 minutes, until soft, squidgy, and translucent slightly, stirring frequently.
4. Tip in the red pepper, garlic, 1 heaped teaspoon of hot chili powder, 1 teaspoon ground cumin and 1 teaspoon paprika.
5. Stir well & cook for 5 minutes, stirring now and then.
6. Brown the lean minced beef. Increase the heat; carefully add the meat to the hot pan & break it up using a spatula or spoon.
7. Continue to stir until all the beef is in uniform, for 5 minutes. Ensure that there are no more pink bits.
8. For Sauce. Crumble 1 beef stock cube in 300ml of hot water. Pour this into the hot pan with the mince mixture.
9. Add a 400g can of chopped tomatoes. Tip in ½ teaspoon dried marjoram, 1 teaspoon sugar and add a good shake of pepper and salt. Squirt in approximately 2 tablespoon of tomato purée; stir well.
10. Gently simmer and bring the mix to a boil; stir well & put a lid on the pan. Decrease the heat and cook for 20 minutes, until it's bubbling gently.
11. Drain & rinse the can of red kidney beans in a sieve & stir them into the chili pot. Bring to the boil again; bubble gently without the lid for 10 minutes, adding a bit of more water, if it looks too dry.
12. Taste the chili & season, if needed.
13. Now replace the lid, turn off the heat and leave your chili to stand for 10 minutes before serving.
14. Serve with soured cream & plain boiled long grain rice.

Chili Mac & Cheese

Prep Time: 50 minutes
Cooking Time: 50 minutes
Servings: 04

Ingredients

- 2 cups macaroni (8 ounces each)
- 1 small red onion, chopped
- 3 garlic cloves, minced
- ½ red bell pepper, chopped
- 8 ounces lean ground beef
- 2 teaspoons chili powder
- 1 teaspoon paprika
- ½ teaspoon dried oregano
- 2 tablespoons tomato paste
- 1 ½ teaspoons cumin
- 2 tablespoons butter
- 1 can diced tomatoes (14.5-ounce), undrained
- 2 tablespoons all-purpose flour
- 1 can kidney beans (15-ounce), undrained
- 2 cups milk
- 4 ounces cream cheese
- 2 cups shredded sharp Cheddar, plus extra for garnish
- 1 teaspoon Dijon mustard
- 3 green onions, chopped
- 1 teaspoon Worcestershire sauce
- 2 tablespoons vegetable oil
- Black pepper and kosher salt

For Serving:
- Corn chips, like Tostitos Scoops

Directions

1. Preheat your oven to 400 F in advance. Fill a large pot with water and bring it to a boil, over moderate heat. Add a bit of salt followed by the macaroni. Cook until al dente. Drain & hold until the cheese sauce is ready.
2. Next, over moderate heat in a medium pot; heat the oil until hot. Add and cook the red onions for a couple of minutes, until soft, covered. Add the bell peppers and garlic; cook for 2 to 5 more minutes; ensure that you don't burn the garlic. Add the ground beef and then, sprinkle with pepper and salt; cook until browned. As you cook the meat; don't forget to stir & break up into small pieces. Once done; add the cumin, chili powder, oregano and paprika; cook until the spices are just fragrant. Add the beans along with their accumulated liquid, tomatoes (with juices), and tomato paste; let simmer for 7 to 10 minutes.
3. Now, over low heat in a large, separate saucepot; heat the butter until melted. Add and cook the flour for a minute, whisking. Whisk in the milk; increase the heat to high & bring the mix to a boil; cook until thickened, whisking. Removing from the heat & whisk in the cheese, cream Cheddar, Worcestershire, mustard and some pepper and salt. Pour the pasta into the cheese sauce; give it a good stir to combine.
4. Mix the chili into the cheese and macaroni. Transfer to a large serving bowl & top with more of Cheddar and green onions. Serve with the corn chips. Enjoy.

Chipotle Pork Chili

Prep Time: 20 minutes
Cooking Time: 20 minutes
Servings: 04

Ingredients

- 1 medium green pepper, chopped
- 3 garlic cloves, minced
- ½ cup salsa
- 1 chipotle pepper in adobo sauce, finely chopped
- 2 teaspoons ground cumin
- 1 small onion, chopped
- 2 teaspoons chili powder
- 1 cup beef broth
- 2 cups cooked pork, shredded
- 1 can red beans (16 ounces), rinsed & drained
- ¼ cup sour cream
- 1 tablespoon canola oil
- Sliced jalapeno pepper, optional

Directions

1. Over moderate heat in a large saucepan; sauté the onion, green pepper, and chipotle pepper in oil for a couple of minutes, until tender. Add & cook the garlic for a minute.
2. Add the beans followed by salsa, broth, chili powder and cumin; bring the mix to a boil, over moderate heat. Decrease the heat & let simmer for 10 minutes, until thickened, uncovered. Add the pork & cook until heated through. Serve with jalapeno slices and sour cream. Enjoy.

Corn & Black Bean Chili

Prep Time: 20 minutes
Cooking Time: 20 minutes
Servings: 08

Ingredients

- 6 Roma (plum) tomatoes, diced
- 1 tablespoon chili powder
- 2 red bell pepper, seeded & chopped
- 1 cup fresh corn kernels
- 1 onion, chopped
- 10 fresh mushrooms, quartered
- 1 jalapeno pepper, seeded and minced
- 1 teaspoon ground black pepper
- 2 cans black beans (15 ounces each), drained & rinsed
- 1 teaspoon ground cumin
- 1 ½ cups chicken broth or vegetable broth
- 1 tablespoon olive oil
- 1 teaspoon salt

Directions

1. Over moderate heat in a large saucepan; heat the olive oil until hot. Sauté the onion, bell pepper, tomatoes, corn, mushrooms, and jalapeño for 10 minutes, until onion turns translucent. Season with cumin, black pepper, and chili powder. Once done; immediately stir in the black beans, broth, and salt; bring the mix to a boil, over moderate heat.
2. Decrease the heat to medium-low. Remove approximately 1 ½ cups of chili to a blender or food processor; purée until completely smooth & stir into the chili again. Serve hot over rice and enjoy.

Firehouse Chili

Prep Time: 20 minutes
Cooking Time: 1 hour & 40 minutes
Servings: 16

Ingredients

- 4 pounds 90% lean ground beef
- 2 tablespoons canola oil
- 1 medium green pepper, chopped
- 2 tablespoons ground coriander
- 4 cans kidney beans (16 ounces each), rinsed & drained
- 2 medium onions, chopped
- 3 cans stewed tomatoes (28 ounces each), cut up
- 1 can beef broth (14 ½ ounces)
- 3 tablespoons chili powder
- 1 teaspoon dried oregano
- 4 garlic cloves, minced
- 2 tablespoons ground cumin

Directions

1. Over moderate heat in a large, Dutch oven; heat the canola oil until hot. Work in batches and brown the beef until no longer pink, crumbling the meat; drain & set aside.
2. Add onions & green pepper; continue cooking until tender. Add the cooked meat back to the Dutch oven. Stir in the leftover ingredients. Bring the mix to a boil. Decrease the heat & let simmer for 1 ½ hours, until flavors are blended, covered.

Frito Pie

Prep Time: 10 minutes
Cooking Time: 30 minutes
Servings: 06

Ingredients

- 2 cans Ranch Style beans (15 ounces each)
- 1 pound ground beef
- 2 cups cheddar cheese, shredded
- 1 medium onion, chopped
- 2 cans enchilada sauce (10 ounces each)
- 1 package Frito corn chips (9 ¼ ounces)
- Green onions, thinly sliced, optional

Directions

1. Preheat your oven to 350 F in advance.
2. Next, over moderate heat in a large skillet; cook the onion and beef until onion is tender and beef is no longer pink, for 6 to 8 minutes; crumbling the meat, as you cook; drain. Stir in the beans & continue to cook until heated through.
3. Reserve approximately 1 cup of corn chips for topping. Place the leftover corn chips in a greased, large baking dish. Layer with the meat mixture, enchilada sauce & cheese; top the kept-aside chips.
4. Bake until the cheese is completely melted, 15 to 20 minutes, uncovered. Just before serving; sprinkle with the green onions. Enjoy.

Lentil Chili

Prep Time: 30 minutes
Cooking Time: 40 minutes
Servings: 06

Ingredients

- 1 large onion, diced
- 4 garlic cloves, minced
- 1 red, yellow, or orange bell pepper, diced
- 2 tablespoons tomato paste
- 1 ½ teaspoons dried oregano
- 2 tablespoons chili powder
- 1 can navy beans or small white beans (15-ounce); don't drain
- ½ teaspoon ground cumin
- 1 tablespoon red wine vinegar
- 4 cups vegetable broth, low sodium
- 1 cup dried brown lentils
- 2 cans fire-roasted tomatoes (14.5-ounces each), diced
- 1 tablespoon olive oil
- Freshly ground black pepper & kosher salt to taste
- 1 dried bay leaf
- Shredded reduced-fat Cheddar, plain yogurt, pickled jalapenos, and crushed tortilla chips, for serving (all are optional)

Directions

1. Over moderate heat in a Dutch oven, heat olive oil until shimmering. Add the onion followed by garlic, bell pepper, several grinds of black pepper and ½ teaspoon salt. Cook for 6 minutes, until vegetables are browned in spots and just tender, stirring occasionally.
2. Stir in the tomato paste, oregano, cumin, and chili powder; continue cooking for 2 more minutes, until fragrant, stirring frequently.
3. Stir in the diced tomatoes, vegetable broth, beans, lentils, bay leaf, a couple grinds of black pepper and ½ teaspoon salt. Bring it to a steady simmer. Once done; decrease the heat to medium-low. Gently simmer for 40 minutes, until the lentils are tender, and the chili has thickened slightly, stirring occasionally, partially covered with a lid.
4. Remove the bay leaf & stir in the vinegar. Season with black pepper and salt. Ladle into individual bowls & serve with the toppings.

Lime Chicken Chili

Prep Time: 20 minutes
Cooking Time: 40 minutes
Servings: 06

Ingredients

- 1 pound ground chicken
- 3 garlic cloves, minced
- 1 tablespoon baking cocoa
- 2 teaspoons ground coriander
- 1 tablespoon all-purpose flour
- ¼ teaspoon pepper
- 1 tablespoon ground cumin
- 2 cans diced tomatoes (14 ½ ounces each), undrained
- 1 medium onion, chopped
- ¼ cup lime juice
- 1 can cannellini beans (15 ounces), rinsed & drained
- 2 flour tortillas (8" each), cut into ¼" strips
- 1 teaspoon lime zest, grated
- 6 tablespoons reduced-fat sour cream
- 1 tablespoon chili powder
- ½ teaspoon garlic pepper blend
- 1 each medium sweet yellow, red, and green pepper, chopped
- 2 tablespoons olive oil
- ½ teaspoon salt

Directions

1. Over moderate heat in a large saucepan, sauté the peppers and onion in hot oil until crisp-tender, for 7 to 8 minutes.
2. Add and cook the garlic for a minute more. Add the chicken; cook & stir until no longer pink, for 8 to 9 minutes, over medium heat.
3. Stir in the flour, seasonings, and cocoa. Add the tomatoes, lime zest and lime juice. Bring the mix to a boil, over moderate heat. Decrease the heat & let simmer until thickened, for 20 to 25 minutes, uncovered, stirring frequently. Stir in the beans & cook until heated through.
4. In the meantime, place the tortilla strips on a large baking sheet lightly coated with the cooking spray. Bake until crisp, for 8 to 10 minutes, at 400 F. Serve the chili with tortilla strips and sour cream. Enjoy.

Meaty Mushroom Chili

Prep Time: 20 minutes
Cooking Time: 1 hour & 10 minutes
Servings: 08

Ingredients

- 1-pound fresh mushrooms, sliced
- 1 cup chopped onion
- 1 pound bulk Italian sausage
- 1 teaspoon sugar
- 1 can V8 juice (46 ounces)
- 1 pound ground beef
- 1 teaspoon dried oregano
- 1 can tomato paste (6 ounces)
- 1 teaspoon Worcestershire sauce
- 1 teaspoon garlic powder
- ½ teaspoon dried basil
- 1 teaspoon salt
- ½ teaspoon pepper

Optional Ingredients:
- Thinly sliced green onions & sour cream

Directions

1. Over moderate heat in a large, Dutch oven; cook the sausage with onion and beef until the meat is no longer pink, for a couple of minutes; drain.
2. Stir in the mushrooms, tomato paste, V8 juice, Worcestershire sauce, sugar, and seasonings. Bring the mix to a boil, over moderate heat. Reduce the heat; cover & let simmer for an hour. Just before serving, top with the sour cream & green onions. Enjoy.

Pepperoni Chili

Prep Time: 20 minutes
Cooking Time: 30 minutes
Servings: 12

Ingredients

- 1 can hot chili beans (16 ounces), undrained
- 2 pounds ground beef
- 1 pound bulk hot Italian sausage
- 1 large green pepper, chopped
- 4 garlic cloves, minced
- 1 can kidney beans (16 ounces), rinsed & drained
- 1 jar salsa (16 ounces)
- 2 teaspoons chili powder
- 1 can pizza sauce (12 ounces)
- 3 cups part-skim mozzarella cheese, shredded
- 1 package sliced pepperoni (8 ounces), halved
- 1 large onion, chopped
- ½ teaspoon pepper
- 1 cup water
- ½ teaspoon salt

Directions

1. Over moderate heat in a large, Dutch oven, cook the sausage with beef, onion, garlic, and green pepper until the meat is no longer pink, for a couple of minutes; drain well.
2. Stir in the beans, salsa, pepperoni, pizza sauce, chili powder, water, pepper, and salt. Bring the mix to a boil. Decrease the heat; cover & let simmer for 20 minutes, until heated through. Sprinkle the servings with cheese and enjoy.

Quinoa Chili

Prep Time: 20 minutes
Cooking Time: 50 minutes
Servings: 08

Ingredients

- 1 small onion chopped
- 3 garlic cloves, minced
- 1 large carrot peeled and chopped
- 2 celery stalks chopped
- 1 green bell pepper chopped
- 1 red kidney beans (15 ounces can), drained & rinsed
- ½ cup quinoa rinsed
- 1 jalapeno pepper diced
- 1 red bell pepper chopped
- 1 medium zucchini chopped
- 2 black beans (15 ounces cans each), drained & rinsed
- 1 can tomato sauce (15 ounce)
- 3 diced tomatoes (15 ounces cans each)
- 1 tablespoon olive oil
- 2-3 tablespoons chili powder depending on your taste
- 1 cup water
- 1 tablespoon ground cumin
- Black pepper & salt to taste

Optional Toppings:
- Green onions, sour cream, cheese, avocado slices, Greek yogurt, crackers, chips, etc.

Directions

1. Over moderate heat in a medium saucepan; mix the quinoa with water; cook for 15 minutes, until water is absorbed; set aside.
2. Next, over moderate heat in a large pot, heat the olive oil until hot. Add and cook the onion for 5 minutes, until tender. Stir in the garlic, carrot, jalapeño, celery, zucchini, and peppers. Cook for 10 minutes, until vegetables are tender.
3. Add the kidney beans, black beans, tomato sauce, and tomatoes. Stir in the cooked quinoa. Season with cumin, chili powder, black pepper, and salt. Let the chili to simmer for 30 minutes, on low.
4. Serve warm; topped with optional toppings and enjoy.

Smokey Peanut Butter Chili

Prep Time: 30 minutes
Cooking Time: 4 hour & 10 minutes
Servings: 12

Ingredients

- 2 ½ pounds lean ground beef (90% lean)
- 1 tablespoon peanut oil or canola oil
- 2 cans green chilies (4 ounces each), chopped
- 1 large green pepper, chopped
- 2 garlic cloves, minced
- 1 large red onion, chopped
- 2 cans (15 ounces each) tomato sauce
- 1 large carrot, peeled and chopped
- 2 cans diced tomatoes with basil, oregano & garlic (14 ½ ounces each), undrained
- 1 to 2 tablespoons ground Ancho chili pepper
- 1 teaspoon smoked paprika
- ½ cup creamy peanut butter
- 1 teaspoon kosher salt

Optional Ingredients:
- Chopped peanuts & shredded smoked cheddar cheese

Directions

1. Over moderate heat in a large skillet; heat the oil until hot; add the beef & cook for 7 to 10 minutes, until no longer pink, breaking it into crumbles. Using a slotted spoon; remove & drain well. Add onion, green pepper, and carrot; cook & stir for 2 minutes, until browned slightly. Add garlic & cook for a minute more. Transfer the vegetables, meat, and drippings to a 6-qt. slow cooker.
2. Stir in the leftover ingredients until mixed well. Cover & cook until vegetables are tender, for 4 hours on low. Just before serving; sprinkle the servings with the peanuts and shredded cheese. Enjoy.

Spiced Apple Chili

Prep Time: 20 minutes
Cooking Time: 2 hours & 30 minutes
Servings: 10

Ingredients

- 3 cups beef broth
- 1 pound ground beef
- 2 tablespoons cider vinegar
- 1 large onion, chopped
- 3 teaspoons chili powder
- 1 can tomato paste (6 ounces)
- 3 teaspoons smoked paprika
- 1 teaspoon ground cinnamon
- 2 garlic cloves, minced
- 1 can chili beans (15 ounces), undrained
- 2 Granny Smith apples, large, peeled & chopped
- ¼ teaspoon pepper
- 2 teaspoons ground cumin
- ½ teaspoon salt

Optional Toppings:
- Diced red onion & shredded white cheddar cheese

Directions

1. Over moderate heat in a large, Dutch oven; cook & crumble the onion with beef for 5 to 7 minutes, until beef is no longer pink; drain.
2. Add the tomato paste, garlic, and spices; cook & stir for 5 minutes, over moderate heat. Stir in the broth and vinegar until blended well. Add the leftover ingredients; bring the mix to a boil. Cover & let simmer for 45 minutes, until flavors are blended & apples are tender, stirring now and then. Serve with your favorite toppings and enjoy.

Sign-up Now
and Be Notified of New Books

Website: readbooks.today

email: juliette@readbooks.today

Printed in Great Britain
by Amazon